THE WELL-DRESSED WOMAN'S DO'S AND DONT'S

THE WELL-DRESSED WOMAN'S DO'S AND DONT'S

BY
ELISE VALLÉE

EBURY
PRESS

First Published in 1925
This edition published in 2008

PRINTED IN GREAT BRITAIN

THE
WELL-DRESSED WOMAN'S
DO'S AND DONT'S

CHAPTER I

THE term "a well-dressed woman" means
far more to-day than just a woman who
wears good or expensive clothes. There is a great
difference between the really well-dressed woman
and one who is merely well clothed—a difference
that can be hardly over-emphasized. To be well
clothed is, of course, already a great deal of an
achievement, but it should not be the end to her
who is ambitious of being well dressed; it is but
one of the stages to that goal which is reached only
when a woman is able truthfully to say to herself :
" I have arrived, as near as it is possible, to Perfection of Appearance."

Now, it is obvious that in order to attain this
ideal, although clothes are of the utmost importance, there are many other things equally essential
to be considered, and this book may be helpful to
those who have not, till now, taken a sufficiently

serious view of the question of appearance as a whole.

In this matter of dress (including, of course, appearance generally) I suppose it will not be denied that the Frenchwoman, and more particularly the Parisienne, holds the undisputed position as the model for women of all other countries. You have all heard and understood the pride in the voice of the woman who tells you that she " is generally taken for a Frenchwoman," and most of you have envied her. We can, therefore, do no better than try to fathom the secret of the Parisienne's unassailable supremacy.

As a matter of fact, there is no mystery in it. It lies in the careful study she gives to the material that Nature has provided before she turns to the question of the trimming with which she will adorn it.

From this point of view the Parisienne may be said to look upon herself as a " Mannequin," which it is her privilege to display to the world as effectively as it is in her power to do. This considered, it becomes plain why clothes, although one of the chief, are not the only means that have to be employed for the attainment of this purpose. Among the contributory means are the proper care of the face, body, and hands, to which, in a great degree, is due the *soignée*, or well-groomed, appearance that is an indispensable part of the effect produced by the well-dressed woman. In addition, there is that serious attention paid to details, without which the best and most expensive of clothes will make little impression.

I cannot repeat too often how important it is to the general result to keep these two points ever before you. Before, therefore, going on to the question of what to wear and when to wear it, I propose to devote a few pages to the subsidiary aspects of the big question, without the study of which no satisfactory results will be achieved.

Now, as " line," in a far greater degree than colour or material, is the all-important problem of our day, we must first consider how to make the best of our figures. This is quite the most difficult question of all to cope with, as the fashion of our time insists that we should all be thin, without allowing us the aid of the helpful, if uncomfortable, stays of our grandmothers.

The universal garment of the present time is the elastic belt. This belt should always be made to measure, and lined in the middle of the front and back with strong coutil, to prevent it " giving " in these important places. It should be fairly

long, and for women with any tendency to stout-
ness should be strengthened with four bones—two
in the front and two at the back. It goes without
saying that it has no opening anywhere, and it
is drawn on upwards from the feet. It should
always be worn next the skin and not over the
chemise.

I may remark that even the naturally thin
woman should not imagine herself immune from
the necessity of at least a light belt ; the most
perfect figure will probably spread in time, and
to be entirely unsupported is tiring, besides
leaving one without the protection against the
cold in winter that the elastic belt affords.

To those who are able to go to Paris for their
things there are hundreds of corset-makers who
make the belt I have described above, such as all
Frenchwomen now wear ; and in London a famous
French firm has a place in Bond Street. There are
doubtless many English firms who would also
make it.

DO'S AND DONT'S

Don't think that in buying smart clothes you
   have done all that is necessary.
Do remember that you have your complexion,
   hair, hands, feet, figure, etc., to attend to.

Don't forget that nothing you put on will look
right until you perfect your " Mannequin."

Don't economize on your elastic belts.

Do wear your belt next your skin. The object
is to appear to be wearing none.

Don't wear it over your chemise ; it will have
bulges, and thus form ugly ridges under
your frock.

Never wash, or have cleaned, elastic belts ; it
destroys the rubber and renders the belt
useless.

CHAPTER III

BEFORE passing on from the preparation of
our " Mannequin " I should like to say
a few words here about the proper care of the face
and hair.

I believe that in England the question of
" Maquillage," or making-up, is still a much-
debated point, and in consideration of this I will
refrain from saying very much about it, except to
mention that it is possible to " make up " without
having in the least a vulgar appearance.

It has been said that " Nature always imitates
Art." In my opinion, unless Nature has given you

a beautiful face you will be wiser to create one for yourself—always provided that you know how to do it, and that the result *is* an improvement when done. However, as I believe that the majority of Englishwomen content themselves with the use of powder and perhaps a lip-stick, I will limit myself to offering you a little advice in the choice of these two important articles.

You should choose a powder of good quality : without, however, being too fine, as this prevents it adhering to the skin and therefore means constant renewal, the result of which being that the shoulders and front of the dress present a perpetually " dusty " appearance. The colour is another important point ; unless you are blessed with the milk-white complexion of the story books, and can support a very light-coloured powder, never use it " neat "—if I may employ the expression ; always mix two or more colours together. For average complexion a mixture of the colours known as " Rachel " and " Naturelle " gives the best results, or for the darker skin that has for some years been the fashion, " Rose " and " Ochre."

When choosing the lip-stick, always avoid those that give a brown or violet tinge to the lips. Though very dark colours are generally considered in better taste, it is a fact that the light shades, if thinly applied, are less noticeable and have a more natural appearance. Never use very greasy lip-salves—they are vulgar looking, and if you so much as take a drink of water will leave marks all over the glass. Indelible lip-colouring can now be had from a few French firms, and I know at least one old-established English firm who makes it.

I do not know if the above information will interest many of my readers, but, at any rate, it is of the utmost importance that all women who want to make a really good appearance should at least pay attention to the care and preservation of the skin.

Given a reasonably healthy complexion to start with, to preserve it successfully it is unnecessary to pour money into the pockets of beauty specialists or to spend a fortune on expensive face creams and lotions. Three things only are required : a cold cream, an astringent lotion, and a little trouble.

An ordinary cold cream, such as any good chemist makes, must be used every night to clean the face of the powder, dust, etc., accumulated during the day. Be sure that the cream is freshly prepared and has not been kept in the shop. When you have rubbed it well in, and wiped it off again with the towel, pat the face briskly, using both hands alternately for five or ten minutes. Then apply the astrigent lotion with a piece of cotton-wool ; the lotion closes the pores of the skin and strengthens the muscles. This done, you can go peacefully to bed, with nothing to do in the morning but wash the face well in cold water. Most women find that the use of soap roughens the skin, and it is quite unnecessary if the face has been well cleaned with cold cream the night before.

The care of the hair is a more individual matter. If your hair is in good condition, it should be sufficient to brush it well every night, and have it shampooed once a fortnight. It is always a good plan to have a " friction " before the hair is dried ; this strengthens the scalp and improves the growth. For the guidance of anyone wishing to change or improve the colour of her hair, let me impress upon her not to be persuaded to try any liquid dyes ; they are often extremely dangerous and sometimes do damage that cannot always be repaired, or only with difficulty. If you must dye your hair, stick to pure henna, which is now available in many different shades.

There is little to say of actual hairdressing. At the present moment every woman's hair is short ; and though the papers sometimes assure us that this craze is nearly over, the evidence of our own eyes contradicts them.

DO'S AND DONT'S

Don't use too fine a powder. Never use a white powder.

Do mix two together to suit the colour of your skin.

Don't use a greasy lip-stick, or one that gives a brown or violet tinge.

Do, if possible, use an indelible one.

Do clean your face thoroughly with cold cream every night.

Don't waste money on expensive " aids to beauty."

Do insist on your cold cream being freshly prepared.

Do use an astringent lotion to prevent wrinkles, etc.

Do wash your face in cold water, and don't use soap.

Don't on any account use liquid dyes, and

Don't dye your hair at all if you can make it look nice without.

Don't say, " My skin is perfect ; it wants nothing

doing to it at all." The day may come
when it will not be quite so perfect, and
you will regret lost time.

CHAPTER III

AND now let us turn from our " Mannequin,"
whom we left clad only in an elastic belt,
to the subject of the under-clothes that she shall
wear.

As each year passes we seem to wear fewer of
the garments that in other times were held to
be of such importance, and of which such amazing
numbers used to be included in the bride's trous-
seau. How many dozens of each article were
considered necessary and how many years of time
and trouble went to their making ! And now we
reduce our under-clothing to the barest necessities.

And yet this apparent frugality is, in reality,
very wise and practical ; for, as we have already
seen, extreme slimness is the only thing that
really matters, and consequently there is no room
to spare under the present-day frocks for bulky
under-garments.

The modern woman has finally cut down this

part of her clothing to two garments only, and these are designed to take up as little space as possible. They consist of a chemise and combinations. Needless to say, the latter has nothing whatever in common with the unattractive object that used to be associated in our minds with the word " combinations." The garment we now wear takes the place of " drawers " and of the little bodice described in sale catalogues as a " camisole." These two things are now combined together to make one, thus avoiding the ungracefulness of the drawers and the rather untidy looking hiatus at the waist.

The " combinations," when well cut, look very like a short frock, and are not at all reminiscent of under-clothes. The simpler the shape the better they are. It is a great mistake to buy these garments ready-made, as the whole effect of daintiness and " chic " is lost if they do not fit the wearer properly. A good shop will, of course, make them to measure for those who can afford the high prices that have to be paid, but a good sewing-maid could easily make them at home, or a woman with a certain amount of leisure could very well manage them herself. These combinations are nearly always made in one piece, slit for a few inches a little below the waist-line each side to allow for a little fullness in the " skirt " and very little in the " bodice." Old-fashioned shaped drawers have practically disappeared, and the " skirt " half of the combinations should be two squares of material, the lower edges held together in the middle back and front by a narrow band, with small buttons passing underneath.

There is not very much to say about the chemise that is worn over the elastic belt and under the combinations. It should be as plain as possible— very much like the old-time vests.

I must not forget to mention the bust bodice that some women find necessary. It is best made in strong net, to be as little noticeable as possible, and should be carefully fitted by the same person who makes the elastic belt.

Very few women wear anything else but silk nowadays for their undergarments, and this habit is by no means as extravagant as it sounds. *Crêpe de Chine* costs no more than we should have to pay now for the fine linen of a few years ago. It is comfortable and pleasant to wear, and extremely easy to wash : an important point in these days when we must all remember the laundry bill. It is worthy of note that the very expensive " heavy " *crêpe de Chine* does not wash as well as the light and cheaper quality. It is better, therefore, to lay out less money on material and renew oftener if necessary.

As regards the trimming of our under-clothes, this is largely a matter of taste. Since the war fine embroidery has rather fallen into disuse and lace has taken its place. For those women who can afford " real " lace nothing is more charming ; but if imitation must be used, a good reproduction only should be allowed. Nothing is in worse taste than a profusion of machine-made lace.

The various types of lace most used at the present time are Malines, Binche, and Point de Paris. For some reasons the fillet and Irish lace that were so popular before the war are now rarely seen.

Though the choice of the colour for under-clothes is also a matter of taste, it is well to remember that rose is always the most satisfactory, as if this colour should be noticed through transparent blouses or summer frocks it will not strike a discordant note, whereas any violent colour will undoubtedly do so. Both blue and mauve are very bad washing colours, and white is completely out of fashion.

I feel that this chapter should not be closed without saying something about stockings, but as silk is now universally worn there is little to mention as regards material, and at the moment of writing we one and all wear the ubiquitous *beige rosée* colour, to which we have remained faithful for day and evening alike.   There is, then, only the question of quality to discuss, and the well-dressed woman rarely diverges from the following rule : The degree of fineness known as " 36 gauge " for morning, " 40 " for afternoon, " 44/50," or even finer qualities, for evening. The woman who cannot be quite so elaborate in her dressing will find the " 36 gauge " a very good all-round quality.

It is not, I am sure, necessary to warn anyone wishing to be well dressed against the wearing of fancy stockings with lace insertions, etc.   They are suitable only for the stage, and are, in any case, unbecoming, as they have the optical effect of thickening the legs.

Silk stockings should be washed in cold water, and with pure Castile soap.   At the first sign of a " ladder " it is always worth sending them to the *stoppeur*, as though this art is not very cheap in England, neither is the present price of silk stockings.

CHAPTER IV

AND now, after many wanderings, we have reached the point where we may drop all minor questions for the enthralling one of actual frocks and hats. And even now, at the eleventh hour, I want to put those off for a few minutes longer while I say a word or two about Fashion.

For fashion is, after all, the most important thing in the choosing of clothes. I suspect that you have all, through the medium of fashion articles and the lips of your artistic friends, received the oft-repeated advice, " Do not be a slave to fashion, but wear what suits you." And now I myself am going to give you a further rule by which to dress, and that is entirely to ignore that piece of advice. I would still more elaborate this remark by saying that *if* you dress in the fashion, you *will*, almost certainly, be wearing what suits you.

All fashions are beautiful—not, perhaps, for the first day or two ; but after we have seen a thing worn a certain number of times *we find it attractive, because our eye becomes accustomed to it*. This must certainly be the secret of the success of the various, often grotesque fashions of the past. How graceless those leg-of-mutton sleeves or bustles seem to us now ; and yet to the bygone wearers they were undoubtedly beautiful, and perhaps even artistic. And therefore I say that all fashions are beautiful. I am excepting, of course, those exaggerated monstrosities that are occasionally offered to us ; but these are never worn by really smart women, and it is, after all, these women that really dictate " the fashion."

Therefore do not conclude that " the fashion does not suit you." Whatever your type it *will* suit you if you learn to wear it properly and arrange for those invisible adaptations that make all the difference.

The Frenchwoman has a system which she refers to as " cheating," by which she means that she will do an infinitesimal something to a frock or hat that will make it more becoming to herself without letting it be seen by her friends that the garment fails to conform, in some small way, to the model that it is essential they should all be wearing on any given occasion.

To know how and when to " cheat " like this is a very great art, and is generally born in one. Some women have not got the natural gift for clothes at all. In such cases I would say, if you are rich, it does not matter very much, as you should put yourself into the hands of one of the great masters of dressmaking, who will give you the benefit of *his* gift ; or if you are not, then you must try very hard to learn it by means of careful thought and study of other women, and I shall, in these pages, do my best to help you.

For instance, if you are too long-waisted—a troublesome thing to be—do not wear your frocks quite as exaggerated in this respect as the present styles decree. Have them made two inches shorter in the waist ; you will then get the same effect, without drawing attention to the shortening of the legs which is always the defect of this fashion, and the serious one in the case of a long-waisted person.

Again, if you are too thin (almost an impossibility in these days), insist on one or two gathers at the shoulders of your frock if it is of the straight-down, chemise type ; it is a small detail, and will not be noticeable, but the slight fullness will prevent that perfectly flat-chested appearance that can be carried too far.

If you are too fat, then a rigid diet is your best stand-by, in conjunction with a deep and well-boned elastic belt. You can also help the fight by having all your clothes cut on the " easy "

2

side—say half an inch larger everywhere than your actual measurements. This prevents any appearance of strain.

These are merely a few examples chosen at random. There are many other little ways in which defects can be concealed without necessitating a departure from the prevailing fashion.

When you say that " the fashion doesn't suit you," you really mean that it accentuates some defect which, if you take sufficient trouble, you ought to be able to overcome, but which you have probably been concealing by the adoption of what you call " a style of your own." If, on the other hand, you have no other reason beyond a preference for this style of dressing, then this book is not for you. If you are a woman past middle-age, then you *ought* to have a style of your own, or you will have no individuality. A young and pretty woman can afford to wear much the same clothes as her young and pretty neighbour, but there is no necessity for all elderly women to look alike, or advantage in doing so.

If you belong to this last category you will not want advice from me ; you will have evolved, through years of experience, the style that is best suited to your type. But to any woman who has still doubts of her own mind let me say one thing :

Do not err on the side of dressing too simply. Extreme simplicity is trying, and becoming only to the young. To the woman whose face is beginning to show her years, hard clothes are a great mistake. Wear things that are soft and a little " important " looking, and avoid cold colours, such as white or grey, which are unbecoming to a complexion that can no longer compete with that of a girl. Don't wear very small hats, but choose a brim that shades the eyes and a discreet trimming that will soften the lines.

But if you are young, I advise you to dress in the fashion ; adapting it, of course, where necessary, to your particular requirements. However becoming your " style " may be, you will never look smart and " in the picture."

In these days when women's clothes are almost a uniform she who does not conform to the model imposed by the really well-dressed women who are to be found in every city, particularly in Paris and London, looks conspicuous, and I am sure you will agree with me that this is never pleasant.

Don't misunderstand me and rush feverishly every season to the openings of the big dressmakers to choose their newest ideas—these are not yet the Fashion, they have yet to be considered and weeded out and tested, until the actual every-

day " Mode " has been decided upon.   Take your
time and watch, and then choose.

CHAPTER V

LET us now look into our wardrobes and
see exactly what the smart, modern woman's
should contain.

A well-dressed woman's requirements to-day
are very different from what they were before the
war.   In those far-off days most people considered
it necessary to have several examples, as different
as possible from each other, of the various garments
that were thought suitable for different occasions.
Women in London and Paris changed their clothes
several times a day before making the final change
for the evening.   Nowadays this custom has
become a thing of the past, and luncheon time
finds us still dressed as we were when we went
out in the morning, and very often we are still
the same, except for a few minor details, when
we go to our rooms to change for dinner.

It is, of course, obvious that the advice given
to the " average " woman does not always apply
to her whose means are considerable, and who,

perhaps, lives a life that necessitates a good deal
of dressing. But it is impossible in one short
book to deal with the needs of many differently
placed people, so I am confining my remarks to
the " average " woman.

The Paris papers at the present moment are
becoming almost hysterical in their denunciation
of an age that has reduced women's clothes, at
any rate in the day-time, to a uniform. They
proclaim with fury that " elegance is dead."
But I do not think this is true. When one sees
two or three exquisitely turned out women entering
a restaurant together, are they any less smart
and attractive because their hats are the same
shape or their dresses the same cut ?   And if we
look at them closely, are we not struck by the way
each one charms us, and stands out from the
others, through the care and originality of the
details of her general effect ?   Let us, then, not
carp at this uniformity, but rather be thankful for
it ; for once we have adopted and adapted it we
know, at any rate, that we look " right."   Also
we cannot ignore the thought of the money
that would have been spent on numerous, and
often superfluous, clothes which is now saved to
us.

It is obviously impossible for me to lay down

definite rules as to the garment that should be
worn by the " average " woman in the day-time,
as this point is entirely dependent on the time
of year and the fashion of the moment.   There is,
however, one very important point that I want to
impress upon you, and I do hope that you will
keep it always before you—*never buy cheap
clothes*.   I am aware that this sounds at first
extravagant and sweeping, but if you think it
over you will soon realize that it is just the opposite.
Buy one good thing in the place of four or five
cheap ones.   Cheap clothes have nothing to
recommend them except their cheapness.   Every-
thing else is against them.   To begin with, there is
never any real style about them—they are the
articles of commerce, not of art.   If they were made
by the masters of the dressmaking trade they would
not be cheap, as the cost of production to these
men, who are artists, is much too great to allow
of their work being sold for a small return.   The
whole success of a cloak or frock is in the " cut,"
and there is never any " cut " in cheap clothes.
In the second place, they do not wear, because
they are made of common and shoddy materials.
The skirts do not " hang," the sleeves wrinkle ;
a shower of rain spots them ; if you sit in them half
an hour they will be creased all over the back.

Again, the colours are crude—for good colours mean good, expensive dyeing, and this cannot be looked for in cheap materials.

If you wear a new frock every time you are seen in public, and it is the work of a small, inferior dressmaker, people will say, " She has always something new on, but she never manages to look well-dressed " ; but if you have one perfect ensemble, they will say, " I have seen her several times in that dress and am always struck by its smartness. I wonder who made it."

At the present time the tailored suit is the most usual for the day-time, and particularly that type known as the " classic," which is again much worn after some years of disfavour ; it is by far the most uesful for those women who are going to include only one tailor-made in their wardrobe. The " classic " suit is always smart and very practical, as it has no elaboration of details or trimming to make it look easily out of date. It must, however, be made by a very good tailor, for if it is not perfectly cut it fails in its object, which is to achieve a masculine neatness and cleanness of line. Needless to say, all the other details, such as hat, shoes, etc., must be carefully chosen to carry out the general scheme. The blouse for the " classic " tailored suit should always be extremely simple, not to say severe. It is generally worn in white, and should be of the shirt description, with pleated front and cuffs fastened with links.

There are women—though not many, I think—for whom the " classic " coat and skirt is too hard in appearance ; but these can usually effect a compromise with a suit a little less severe in cut while still remaining very simple, and softened with fur collar and cuffs.

If the coat and skirt are ordered from a first-class house and great care is taken to make it perfect, one can be easily made to last a year, or even longer, for the woman who cannot afford to renew it often. It is a very good plan to make a habit of ordering a tailored suit in the spring, of not too heavy material, and wear it at once as long as you like ; it can then be worn again in the autumn and winter with the addition of a woolly coat or warm waistcoat underneath. The Frenchwoman usually wears her coat and skirt, at any rate for mornings, all through the early summer months up to the time of her departure for the country. This is much to be recommended, as the habit of some Englishwomen of wearing light country frocks in London is deplorable, being the reverse of smart and in bad taste. Every kind of frock has its own occasion, and country clothes are no more suitable to town than town ones are to country.

Tailor-made suits should never be worn in decided colours, but always in black, grey, brown, etc., according to the prevailing fashion. The really smart woman at the present moment first chooses her suit in a neutral colour and then matches her hat, shoes, handbag, and umbrella to go with it, and as this gives a very *soignée*, well-finished appearance, I do not think it will go out of fashion for some time.

Black has been for a long time the universal colour for the day-time, but for the tailored suit brown or dark grey is better if the suit is to do duty for some time, as black has a tendency to become shiny at the seams and assume an unpleasant greenish tinge. A plain material is always more practical than a fancy one, because patterns go out of fashion, and one also gets very tired of them in a thing that is to be worn every day.

DO'S AND DONT'S

Don't have a lot of clothes for the same kind of occasion ; it is extravagant and unnecessary.

Never buy cheap clothes ; they are also extravagant and dowdy as well.

Do have a tailored suit in your wardrobe, and
be sure it is the best of its kind, also

Do, unless it is particularly unbecoming to you,
adopt the " classic " shape.

Do go to a first-class tailor.

Do, in your suits, as in all other matters of dress,
devote much care and thought to the details.

Don't wear country clothes in town.

Don't order coloured suits, unless very dark
ones, and

Don't choose patterns unless you are going to
have several tailor-mades.

CHAPTER VI

IN our study of day-clothes, before we can
go on to the subject of dresses, we must first
consider the coats that are to be worn over them.
This naturally brings us to the question of the
fur coat, and a very important question it is.

The fur coat is, and always has been, something
of a white elephant. It is a necessary part
of every woman's wardrobe, but it is very

expensive to buy, and, what is worse, it is a continuous expense for it is never paid for. Whatever shape you choose for your fur coat one year it is quite certain that you will want it wider or narrower, longer or shorter, the year after ; according to the needs that fashion has imposed upon you, and then the trouble begins. You cannot wear it as it is, for there is nothing in this world as hopelessly dowdy as an out-of-date fur coat, and therefore you are launched on the endless expense of " transforming." This process has to be gone through every year and costs a great deal of money, as fur work is very highly paid, particularly since the war. Moreover, the furrier always has to add skins to make the model you choose ; he has never been known to have too much of your fur in hand.

At the risk of sounding inconsiderate of my readers' pockets I must here repeat the advice " not to buy cheap," as this applies to fur as much as to anything else. Apart from the obvious reason that a cheap fur coat cannot be effective, it is an established fact that the less costly fur is quite as expensive in the end, because to divert attention from its unluxurious appearance the skins are generally made up into an ultra-elaborate model, and therefore the coat, to satisfy the demands of fashion, will have to submit to the above-mentioned " transformation " process a great deal oftener than would the " classic " model which we find in fur coats quite as often as in tailored suits.

So you will see that I am pleading for the furs that may be called " precious." Fashion, for several years now, has required every really smart woman to own a long coat of kolinsky or mink (sable is nowadays only for the wealthy), and if you can manage to provide yourself with one of these your troubles are over, as regards fur coats, at any rate. You will choose the " classic " model, that is to say, of straight cut, fairly full, to wrap round comfortably, and of ankle length. This model is not affected by the whims of fashion, and its whole beauty lies in the luxury of the fur ; these precious skins are hardly ever made up into fancy shapes.

The alterations that the " classic " coat may occasionally need are very slight—perhaps a little difference in the shape of the collar, or a little more or less fullness in the skirt : and, needless to say, the width that you may one day have taken out will be carefully preserved for the day when you may wish to put it in again . Beyond the renewal of the lining from time to time, this is the extent of the trouble that you need expect from the " precious " fur coat.

The choice of the fur is not a very difficult matter, as there are not many to choose from. As I have already said, sable is usually out of the question, and kolinsky is not a good investment, as it wears very badly, and, being a dyed fur, it turns reddish after a time from exposure to the sun, etc. I personally recommend mink, which is undyed, very beautiful if the skins are well matched, and will wear indefinitely if a reasonable amount of care is taken to preserve the coat from moth and like dangers.

One of the greatest advantages to be appreciated in possessing a " precious " fur coat is that it is worn indifferently with day or evening clothes. What used to be called " opera cloaks " are now completely out of fashion and are never worn except by those people who are not the fortunate owners of a " precious " fur coat. In the big Paris restaurants and theatres you will see one smart woman after another entering wrapped in a mink or kolinsky coat. Chinchilla is another very attractive fur, but it has many disadvantages : its price is practically prohibitive, it does not wear at all, and it is entirely unsuited to the day-time. The same criticism applies to ermine.

In ordering a valuable fur coat it is better not to choose a model in which the skins are worked to form a complicated pattern ; for though the effect is sometimes pretty, to be saddled with a garment composed of zigzagging lines would be awkward if very plain working should be worn the next year. The tails of the animal as trimmings are not now used at all.

For the lining of a valuable coat do not have colours. This type of fur needs no embellishment, and should always be lined with a good quality plain silk, matched as closely as possible to the colour of the skins.

Those who are forced to content themselves with a less expensive type of coat have more variety in the choice of skins ; but these cannot, on the other hand, be worn as evening cloaks. Moleskin is pretty, but wears exceptionally badly ; beaver wears better, but is not a very good investment, as it came into fashion a short time ago and is now practically out again, and it is difficult to say whether it will be popular in the future. Moleskin is better in this latter respect, as it it is what we may call a "standard" fur. In the same category is squirrel, which, under the name of *petit-gris*, is much worn in France. This is a very good wearing fur, is not exorbitant in price, and is soft and becoming. Sealskin and seal musquash are good, dependable furs, but they are very little worn just now.

To the woman who cannot afford a good fur coat at all my advice is to get from a first-rate house a really smart fur-trimmed coat. These coats look very nice for afternoon wear, and should be made of satin or other material that fashion dictates. A virtue may be made of necessity by matching them to the frock that is to be worn underneath. This type of coat is usually made in black, and as long as such things are worn at all they will probably continue to be if not in black, at least in dark greys or browns, colours suitable in a garment that is to do duty as a fur coat.

I should like to take this opportunity to say a word or two about the choice of colours generally.

For some years now smart women have worn nothing but black, at any rate in the day-time; and this persistent fashion is sometimes criticized as giving an unnecessarily funereal appearance, as well as being deprecated by many as being ageing. Ageing it is not; in my opinion the younger the woman, the better she looks in black.

As fashions come from Paris it is not surprising that women should have adopted black for the day-time, as no smart Frenchwoman would be seen wearing colours in the street. Colours make the wearer too conspicuous, and the well-dressed woman should keep them for the country. To the majority of women black is the most becoming thing to wear ; it makes a neutral background for the delicate tints of the face, while light-coloured clothes, on the other hand, in drawing attention to themselves, detract from the face.

In nine cases out of ten the woman who thinks that black does not suit her is not following the right methods with her complexion. She is using the wrong coloured powder, or presenting to the world a face bare of artificial aids when she really needs them. The well-dressed woman who is sure of her " Mannequin " should wear dark clothes in the street and keep colours for indoor occasions, when she will have the advantage of a softer and more becoming light.

DO'S AND DONT'S

Don't be hasty in the purchase of fur coats.

Don't buy cheap fur, and never buy imitations.

Do, if possible, have one coat only, but have it of " precious " fur.

Don't choose a fancy or elaborate shape, and

Don't have bright linings.

Don't choose chinchilla or ermine, unless you can afford another coat for day-time as well.

Don't wear an " opera cloak " if you have a valuable fur coat.

Don't, at the present time, have your coat trimmed with tails ; they are the hall-mark of the dowdy.

Don't buy moleskin if you want it to last more than two winters, and don't be surprised if it is shabby at the end of one.

Never give your fur coat to be altered to a furrier that you have not a thorough personal knowledge of, or a very high recommendation to from a friend.

Do wear dark colours in the street.

Don't say black doesn't suit you until you have tried a black dress with your face skin as near perfection as you can make it.

CHAPTER VII

HAVING decided the vexed question of the fur coat, let us now consider the frock to be worn beneath it in winter, or, without a coat perhaps, in summer.

These frocks are what the French refer to as "little dresses," the reason being that they are very simple and young looking, and should have as little elaboration of frills and drapery as possible, so that there is nothing to be crushed by the weight of the coat or, if worn uncovered in the summer, their wearers may not look overdressed. I should like to draw your attention here to a very important point, namely, that no well-dressed woman should ever be seen in the street without something over her dress. The present custom, an incongruous one, is, whatever the heat of the day, to wear a fur over the shoulders.

For some time now this fur has been strictly limited to the various types of "fox," and I am inclined to think this fashion will continue, as stoles, capes, etc., are long since out of date. The recent revival of the coloured scarf, though a pretty novelty, was too quickly taken up and produced in cheap materials, and consequently the smart woman returned to her fur.

The choice of the fur again depends on the purse. It is the ambition of every well-dressed woman to wear a "silver" or "blue" fox, and they are both very beautiful, but, as is the case with so many of the valuable furs, they are dreadfully expensive and do not wear well. A much-used compromise is the animal known in England as the " cross " fox, and it is not ineffective if a fair price is paid for it. There are, of course, many cheaper fox furs, such as " red," " grey," " black," and " white " fox, but, in my opinion, if one cannot afford better than these, one is wiser to go without, and to turn the dress into a " three-piece frock," with a light coat worn over the dress.

As we have already seen, bright or light colours are not permissible for the street, so the choice of the frock must be made among the darker shades. Here, again, black takes the centre of the stage. At last, however, the rigid rule that forbade even the slightest colour relief is lifted, and coloured or metal embroideries play a big part in the beautifying of our " little dresses."

The average woman will need about three of these frocks, though she who has limited means can very well do with less. The most sensible thing is to order two in the early spring and wear them alternately, or as occasion requires ; then, on returning to town in the autumn, if one of them is not as fresh as the other, it will do excellently for everyday wear and the other for luncheon or tea.

The Frenchwoman always has a third, or if

she has only two she keeps one for evenings, as so great a part of French life is spent nowadays in restaurants, and the smart Frenchwoman rarely dresses on these occasions. I believe that English-women are beginning to adopt this habit, and it seems to me to have much to recommend it. A woman in a low dress or without a hat is rather conspicuous in a restaurant where evening dress is not a rule, and the clothes that are correct for a gathering in a private house are not really suitable for a public place.

If you want to be smart wear a really good frock with long or short sleeves, of satin or *crêpe de Chine*, as the fashion dictates, under a fur coat, or with furs round the shoulders according to the season.

To the majority of women a " model " frock is the height of luxury. In principle I am of the same opinion, as you may be sure that the best of the creator's art has gone to the making of it ; but you must not lose sight of the fact that the " model " frock is only for the woman who can claim to be truly what is called " stock size." If you are not of this enviable shape leave " models " strictly alone, for alteration always ruins them. In letting them out here and taking them in there, in lengthening and shortening and pinching and stretching you ruin the line, which is generally their greatest claim to beauty. It is usually better for the maker of the model to reproduce it to fit you, adapted where necessary to your individual requirements, or, if you cannot afford to be dressed by the big French dressmakers, go to a good firm that buys *good French models* and copies them for their clients.

When you have found your dressmakers let me impress upon you to stick to them, and not to be led away by the " discoveries " and passing enthusiasms of your less faithful friends. It is a fatal thing to be always trying new dressmakers, as each one is bound to need a little time to get used to your type and learn how best to suit it. If you are always changing dressmakers they will always be in the preliminary stages, in which the best results cannot be expected.

Don't, when big firms have " sales of models," rush to pick up bargains without thinking of what you are doing. The same drawbacks will apply to them as are mentioned above, and, moreover, they are usually in a bad state of preservation. A dress that has been put on and taken off by the mannequin several times a day during a whole season is bound to get torn and damaged, and, though cheap, when brought home in triumph is often found to be beyond repair. Also, these " bargains " are often very dirty. Never wear a dress of this kind without first sending it to the cleaner. If you think the matter over you will see that to omit this precaution is, to say the least, unhygienic.

I do not deny, however, that there are sometimes opportunities of securing a really good dress for a small sum. If you are a client of the firm they will generally send you a line to inform you when they are going to dispose of their models, so that you may go at once and take the first choice. You may then find something worth having that is being sacrificed only with the object of making room for the new models.

DO'S AND DONT'S

Never go out in the street without a coat or fur or some sort of wrap over your frock.

Don't wear cheap imitation foxes ; substitute a coat or cape if you cannot afford good furs.

Don't wear colours in the street.

Don't, as a general rule, wear low dresses to dine in restaurants, or, if you do, never leave your cloak in the cloak-room.

Don't buy " model " frocks, unless you are really
  " stock size."

Do make sure a dress is worth having before you
  buy a bargain.

Do have it cleaned before you wear it.

Don't change your dressmaker when you have
found a really good one.

CHAPTER VIII

THE question of hats, dear to every woman's
heart, is not an easy one to approach, as
it is so dependent on the fashion of the moment,
but I should like to make a few remarks about
hats here.

First of all, in the matter of hats there is considerable scope for " cheating," as, though the
hat must, of course, conform to the prevailing
fashion, it is equally necessary that it should be
becoming to the wearer.

Nowadays hats are generally small, and whatever the changes of each successive season, they
do not bring us back the huge hat of ten or fifteen
years ago. Now, small hats, though to my way
of thinking, smarter, as they give a small, neat

shape to the head, are by no means becoming to every one. They never suit a woman with a full, heavy face. The woman of this type should have her hats made rather loose round the forehead. It is a great mistake to have them tight, as they frequently give the effect of a face bulging out beneath the hat. Here is a useful hint as to how to " cheat " in wearing a small hat. Have what the French call the *tour de tête* (I use this term as I know of no English equivalent, but it really means " the size round the head at the top of the brim ") made to fit you comfortably, and then, when the crown is put on, have it made a tiny bit too large for the hat, as it were. By too large I mean too wide all round, and by this means you will have a crown wide enough not to be trying to a full face while at the same time preserving the actual dimensions imposed by the smart hat.

Never let the person who makes your hats send you home one in which the crown is narrower at the base than at the top ; this will give the crown, in the front especially, a sloping back appearance, instead of the straight one it should have. The latter fault makes the nose look big, and is disastrously unbecoming to every type of face. Avoid much-trimmed hats, for in hats, as in clothes, the line is the important thing.

I have spoken above of " the person who makes your hats," and it may be necessary to explain that no smart woman now buys her hats ready made. They are always specially made and carefully fitted for the wearer. Your milliner must be selected with care, and only from the best available. She must know her art thoroughly and have intelligence and understanding to study and display to the best advantage the lines of each separate client's head. Again, let me warn you against constant changing of your milliner—change till you find the right one, and then never change again.

During the time that we are allowed a certain amount of licence in the shape of the brims of our hats it is well to remember these few points : If you have a tendency to a double chin don't wear a mushroom-shaped brim that fits tightly all round the head, concealing the ears and eyes ; this will emphasize your weak point. Have your brim shaped to a right angle from your crown, and not straight down.

If you have a prominent nose don't wear your brim turned up at the side ; it will give you an ugly profile. Don't, unless there should be a complete revolution in the present-day fashions, wear your hats perched high on your head. The crown of the hat should enclose the whole head smoothly, like a cap, coming down almost to the nape of the neck at the back, and covering, or coming just down to, the eyebrows in front.   (The latter is particularly important for the woman with a high forehead.)

If you have a very flat-shaped head behind don't wear a hat turned up sharply at the back, to draw attention to the defect.   By the intelligent manipulation of the lines of brim or crown all bad points can be at least toned down, if not concealed altogether.

Of colour there is little to say, as one cannot predict what will be worn for more than a few months ahead.   It is sufficient to say that black is usually the favourite and the most becoming, though at the moment many of the smartest women have the hat made to match perfectly the frock with which it is to be worn.   This is, I think, a happy idea, and gives a very well-finished appearance.

Coloured hats are rarely smart in town, and white is unbecoming to all but the woman with a perfect ivory complexion.   In addition, it always manages somehow to look over-dressed.   Whatever the simplicity or lack of trimming of the hat itself, however, white is almost exclusively worn for the Riviera or summer resorts.   But take my advice and don't sacrifice your complexion to it if you are one of those whom it does not suit.

DO'S AND DONT'S

Do have your hats made to measure.

Do have a really good milliner, and

Don't change your milliner.

Do wear a brim shaped to flatter your face.

Don't wear a narrow crown unless your face is pointed.

Don't wear your hat perched on top of your head.

Don't wear a tight hat if you have a full face.

CHAPTER IX

I SUPPOSE that to the average Englishwoman the corner of her wardrobe containing her evening frocks is the most interesting.   There are probably half a dozen there, each tied up in its linen bag.   In the Frenchwoman's cupboard will be found two or three at the most.

As I have already mentioned elsewhere, the

Frenchwoman never wears an evening dress except to go to a dance or supper at some well-known dancing-place. It is also true, as I have said, that smart Englishwomen are adopting this custom.

Of the elaborate frocks that used to be called ball-dresses I shall have nothing to say, since for the woman to whom this book is addressed they will have little interest. It is a mistake to have an exaggerated number of dresses of this type, as they cost a great deal of money ; and unless the wearer is likely to go a lot into rather formal society they are quite unnecessary.

The simple evening frock that is suitable for a private dinner or a small private or restaurant dance—in fact, almost any evening occasion—is of much greater importance. The number to have is determined by the amount of wear that will be expected from them ; three or four is generally sufficient. They must be very perfect of line, especially for dancing, and the simpler they are the better. Perfection of simplicity is the ideal of dressing of our day—that almost Spartan simplicity of line and trimming that is so difficult to achieve, and can be found, as a rule, only in the best dressmaking houses.

The present-day evening frocks are really duplicates of our day frocks made in more expensive

materials, and a little more cut out under the arm
and at the neck. The fashion for very low-cut
evening dresses went out a few years ago, and does
not look like coming back again. The smart
woman barely shows her neck below the throat
line in the front, and only a little more in the back.
It is a curious fashion making an impression
almost of prudishness, but it is a great deal
prettier than the exaggerated display of chest,
and especially of back, of a few years ago.

The smart woman in the evening has always one
difficulty to overcome, and that is not to look
theatrical. You will notice that stage favourites
are hardly ever seen in day clothes. If you drift
casually into almost any theatre you will catch
sight of the inevitable " star " in an elaborate
evening dress ; or if you see her dining or supping
at a restaurant she is probably wearing a similar
dress. The problem of the well-dressed woman
is to be smart without looking " stagey." I
think it was probably this necessity which was
the origin of the simple evening dress and which
accounts for its popularity.

The dress is simple only in form, rarely in
material. It is generally made in the richest
metal tissues and brocades in gold and silver. If
a plain material is chosen it is entirely covered

with such elaborate embroideries that the background can hardly be seen. All these details are, however, very much a matter of fashion, and though they appear to be firmly established for a long time to come we cannot say for certain.

In colour I am prevented by the same reason from giving any definite advice. The frock of all one colour is, in any case, not a good investment. It " dates " the dress, and the wearer gets very tired of it. Gold or silver, black or white, or black-and-white, is really smarter than colours. The well-dressed Frenchwoman is nowadays rarely seen in anything deviating from this self-imposed rule.

Let us say, for the sake of argument, that you are contemplating ordering four simple evening frocks. If you have a very decided love for colour, just one in blue or green, or whatever your preference is, but not more. The probability is that your dresses will be identical in shape, and each must therefore be given its individuality through the choice of material and the charm of carefully-thought-out details.

These details are not confined to the arrangements of a drapery or the design of an embroidery. There is a great deal of responsibility that lies, not with the dressmaker, but with the prospective wearer during that important hour when she is dressing to go out.

Of shoes, etc., I shall be writing farther on, but this seems a good moment to give a few hints as to the jewels to be worn.

In these times, when to live at all is so painfully expensive, the woman who can go out and buy a new jewel whenever an attractive idea is launched, is rare ; but if you cannot offer yourself the latest creations from Cartier you can, at least, avoid wearing out-of-date jewellery. You can do this either by putting it away altogether or by exchanging several old-fashioned pieces for one new one. Of course, in the case of family " heirlooms " this is not feasible ; but, then, if there is no objection to it, they can be reset at comparatively little cost, and this is always worth doing if the jewels are really out of date. One must give the work to a thoroughly trustworthy person, and choose the designs for the settings with care, avoiding any exaggerations of fashion.

It is the ambition of every smart woman, whatever her nationality, to wear a string, or strings, of pearls ; and it is an amazing thing that, in spite of circumstances, most of us seem somehow or other to realize this ambition. Pearls are essential, as an accessory of dress, to our modern ideas, and the woman who does not possess any had better sacrifice most of the jewellery she has acquired from time to time and exchange it for a string, large or small, according to the capital in hand.

It is a comfort to know that the " rope of pearls " falling below the waist is no longer imperative ; a short string of fair-sized pearls encircling the throat, or two or more smaller ones, will do quite as well. The Frenchwoman never removes her pearls, except to sleep, though she keeps them concealed under her dress till fairly late in the afternoon.

The pendant is an article of jewellery that has entirely disappeared from fashion, and anyone possessing several of these ornaments can with a clear conscience exchange them for pearls. Brooches and bangles, which have also not been very much worn of late years, are now coming fast into favour again.

As to rings, the well-dressed woman can hardly do without one good one on each hand. If she should be the happy possessor of a big uncut emerald or diamond, this, worn on the third finger of the right hand, should be sufficient. Gold wedding rings, by the way, are being replaced by a narrow band of platinum studded all round with any precious stone—diamonds usually.

Try and avoid, if possible, having jewels all of
different colours, as nothing is more ugly or in
worse taste than rubies, sapphires, emeralds,
etc., all worn together. Diamonds, pearls, and
emeralds are safest, and in my opinion the most
beautiful. Fine emeralds, however, cost small
fortunes. Sapphires, if dark and worn with
diamonds, are effective, and are less expensive.

DO'S AND DONT'S

Don't fill your wardrobe with expensive and
  elaborate evening dresses.

Do have simple frocks, and not a great many
  of them.

Don't have more coloured dresses than you can
  help.

Do be careful that they should not look theatrical.

Don't think when dressing that your frock only
  is important ; study your jewels as well.

Don't wear out-of-date jewellery ; if there is
  no objection, have it reset by a really good
  firm.

Don't wear a mass of jewels ; have a few good
  ones.

Don't wear several different-coloured stones
  together.

4

CHAPTER X

OUR grandmothers used to say that "a lady is known by her hands and her feet," and there is certainly much truth in the assertion. It is equally sound criticism nowadays to judge a well-dressed woman by her gloves and shoes.

No woman can be smart unless her feet are perfectly dressed, but they cannot be perfectly dressed unless they are also perfectly looked after. Before ordering shoes, unless you are that blessed being "who never suffers from her feet," first be sure that you have a good chiropodist. Shoes become more elaborate every year, and consequently more and more difficult to wear with comfort. The woman who is vain of her feet (as every woman should be) and wants to wear smart shoes, will be wise to visit the chiropodist once a month, or in some cases even oftener.

The next thing to do is to find, and to keep to, a first-class bootmaker. Ready-made shoes are never smart, and are generally uncomfortable. The criticisms that I have applied to ready-made clothes apply also to ready-made shoes : they have no style and they do not wear well. In the case of shoes, to wear badly is a particularly undesirable fault, as they do not change in fashion every other minute, or, at any rate, not so much as to make a last season's pair out of the question for this season's wearing ; but they will be of no use to anyone if they are worn out.

Since the war women have worn nothing else but patent leather in town ; but happily this is now going out of fashion again. I say happily, because there is no leather so trying even to the strongest feet, and, also, patent leather nowadays is often not patent leather at all, or of such poor quality that it cracks in a week or two. Brown box calf or kid are taking its place for mornings, and the last named is in every way to be recommended, as it looks nice and wears indefinitely.

Suède and Antelope are appearing again for afternoons, and for evening gold or silver are the established favourites. A very useful hint is to keep these, when not in use, always wrapped in grease-proof paper ; this will prevent them tarnishing. It is essential to have one pair of black satin shoes to wear for restaurants, etc., when not in evening dress. Brown suède or calf are most suitable for the country, and white for the Riviera.

It is important to choose carefully the shape to be adopted before the bootmaker makes you a last, and not to pass the first pair until they

are really comfortable. Once you are satisfied
you have only to order what you need in different
materials, and are saved all the misery and disap-
pointment of trying on countless different ready-
made shoes. As we have seen in studying other
details of the well-dressed woman's outfit, it
costs no more to buy good things occasionally
than cheap things often.

Do not wear low-heeled shoes simply because
you think that those with high heels are unhealthy.
Many doctors uphold the latter and condemn
low heels as unhealthy. Low heels are certainly
very tiring to the arch of the foot, and give it a
particularly ugly, flat-footed appearance. Also,
whatever anyone tells you, they are never smart.

I may add that people with tender feet, inclined
to corns and chilblains, should avoid the shape
known as the " court shoe." It is better to have
some kind of a strap as a support to the instep.
Pointed toes are also a mistake, but, fortunately,
at the moment they are not in fashion.   The shape
now universally worn by all smart women is
perfectly comfortable if made by a good bootmaker and on a satisfactory last. It will be
obvious that there are as many opportunities for
" cheating " with shoes as there are with clothes.
For instance, if you have very flat feet the higher

the heels you wear the better. (It goes without
saying that the same thing applies to the woman
who suffers from being too short.) Again, if
your feet are large you should see that the fronts
of your shoes, called by the bootmaker the
vamps, are cut very short with the opening well
rounded ; this will, in appearance, halve the
length of your feet.

The remaining accessory to a well-dressed
woman's clothes—gloves—does not give me much
scope for advice. For morning or afternoon in
town they are generally of suède or buckskin,
and at the present time are nearly always worn
to match exactly in colour the accompanying
dress. With a tailored suit some women wear
wash-leather ; but these are really more suitable
for the country, where they are imperative. White
kid gloves are entirely out of fashion, and suède in
pale colours takes their place. Gloves with
evening dress are now never seen. No woman is
well dressed unless her gloves are well chosen
and spotless. I am aware that this is not always
easy for the woman whose means are limited,
and she would perhaps be wise to make a habit
of wearing wash-leather for the mornings. Many
people find the new washable suède gloves satisfactory, though I am not a great believer in them

myself. If, however, you should decide on these, remember that it is never wise to choose them in light colours, as they become several shades lighter with washing. These gloves are best washed in household soap and lukewarm water or cold water, and should be dried very slowly away from artificial heat.

I shall not attempt to describe the remaining details of the smart woman, such as handkerchiefs, handbag, umbrella, etc., as they would probably be out of date long before this little book is in print; but I would remind you that these, as other details, are important, and care must be exercised in the choosing of them.

To sum up, the chief rules for a well-dressed woman are these : To make the best you possibly can of your face and figure before starting to dress them at all. Never to waste money on cheap clothes, shoes, hats, etc., but rather to buy a few really good things every year. To take trouble and use your intelligence in the choosing of your clothes, and to take good care of them when you have got them.